## Congressional Research Service
### Informing the legislative debate since 1914 _____

# Legislation Proposed to Implement the U.S.-Mexico Transboundary Hydrocarbons Agreement

**Curry L. Hagerty**
Specialist in Energy and Natural Resources Policy

**James C. Uzel**
Geospatial Information Systems Analyst

November 6, 2013

Congressional Research Service

7-5700

www.crs.gov

R43204

# Summary

The offshore areas of the Gulf of Mexico provide a setting for domestic and international energy production, U.S. military training and border operations, trade and commerce, fishing, tourist attractions, and recreation. These governmental, commercial, and cultural activities depend on healthy and productive marine and coastal areas for a range of economic and social benefits. Consequences of hurricanes and oil spills demonstrate that offshore areas in the Gulf of Mexico are governed by a number of interrelated legal regimes, including treaties and international, federal, and state laws.

A key congressional interest has been the federal role in managing energy resources in deepwater areas of the Gulf of Mexico, particularly in waters beyond the U.S. exclusive economic zone (EEZ), more than 200 miles from shore. In 2012, the United States and Mexico signed an agreement known as the U.S.-Mexico Transboundary Hydrocarbons Agreement (the Agreement). This Agreement could mark the start of an energy partnership in an area of international waters that the U.S. Department of the Interior's (DOI's) Bureau of Ocean Energy Management (BOEM) estimates to contain as much as 172 million barrels of oil and 304 billion cubic feet of natural gas. The main purposes of the partnership would be to lift a moratorium and to jointly develop reservoirs of oil and natural gas, referred to as "transboundary resources," that exist in areas straddling the marine border of both countries. The Agreement stems from a series of bilateral treaties originating in the 1970s. Like other diplomatic measures, for the Agreement to take effect, it must be placed before each country's national lawmakers for review. To date, Mexico has completed review and accepted the Agreement. The Agreement awaits the passage of implementing legislation in the U.S. Congress.

In the United States, implementing legislation involves the two main commitments of the Agreement. First, under the Agreement, the two countries establish a framework for jointly developing 1.5 million acres along a 550-mile border. Diplomats on both sides of the border claim that this framework achieves a mutual goal of greater options for energy production to help gain greater energy independence for both countries. A concurrent commitment is to dismantle a treaty-based moratorium on oil and gas development agreed to in 2000, encompassing 158,584 acres along a 135-mile portion of the border. Current treaty provisions establish that the ban will expire in 2014.

Implementing the Agreement faces hurdles in both countries. In the United States, among other hurdles, is the transitional status of U.S. safety reforms announced after the 2010 *Deepwater Horizon* spill. These reforms are being phased in and full implementation is not anticipated until later in 2013 and 2014. These regulations are considered by industry and U.S. regulators to be a more robust set of deepwater drilling standards than were in place prior to the *Deepwater Horizon* spill. Until they take full effect, the treaty-based moratorium is perceived by many as a necessary mechanism to protect against the risk of oil spills. In Mexico, although the Agreement has been accepted, implementation poses various constitutional and regulatory challenges.

U.S. legislation to approve and implement the Agreement includes H.R. 1613 and S. 812. On June 27, 2013, the House passed H.R. 1613 (H.Rept. 113-101). On October 14, 2013, the Senate passed S. 812. Absent a deadline for U.S. approval of the Agreement and consideration of implementing legislation, if any, it is difficult to predict the timing of further legislative action. Many in Congress have expressed the view that the expiration of the moratorium in 2014 will prove a catalyst for legislative attention during the remainder of the 113th Congress.

# Contents

# Figures

# Appendixes

# Contacts

# Introduction

Since the 1970s, prompted by high fuel prices and a mutual interest in greater energy security, the United States and Mexico have agreed to a series of bilateral treaties defining territorial claims and laying the groundwork for future oil and gas development partnerships. These treaties and other diplomatic activities are helping to define each nation's stake in oil and gas resources in ocean areas in the western Gulf of Mexico beyond each country's 200-mile exclusive economic zone (EEZ).[1]

A prominent component of these treaties has been an offshore moratorium on oil and gas development covering a 158,584-acre area within a larger transboundary area encompassing 1.5 million acres.[2] The stated purpose of this moratorium is to allow time for both countries to form a partnership for jointly developing transboundary oil and gas resources beyond each country's EEZ.

The United States and Mexico are moving to form a partnership to jointly manage areas for offshore drilling operations. This entails lifting the temporary moratorium and replacing it with a framework for a joint development scenario.[3] The United States and Mexico are not alone in seeking this type of energy partnership. Around the world, nations claiming ocean areas beyond established national borders are forming similar partnerships to cope with challenges associated with managing offshore areas for developing oil and gas resources.[4] The global race for ocean energy resources is among other contributors to the intensification of diplomatic talks between the United States and Mexico that started in 2010. These talks were concluded in 2012 by both countries signing the U.S.-Mexico Transboundary Hydrocarbons Agreement (the Agreement).[5]

Several hurdles stand in the way of this energy partnership — each stemming from different policy dilemmas on each side of the border.[6] While the Mexican Senate moved swiftly to approve the Agreement on April 12, 2012, and the Mexican Presidency completed other domestic requirements on May 22, 2012, uncertainties surround Mexico's implementation of the

---

[1] See *Treaty to Resolve the International Boundary*, signed on November 23, 1970; *Treaty on Maritime Boundaries between the United Mexican States and the United States of America*, signed on May 4, 1978; and *Treaty between the Government of the United Mexican States and the Government of the United States of America on the Continental Shelf*, signed on June 9, 2000.

[2] For legal jurisdictions related to ocean energy development, see CRS Report RL33404, *Offshore Oil and Gas Development: Legal Framework*, by Adam Vann.

[3] Under the U.S.-Mexico Transboundary Hydrocarbons Agreement, both countries might proceed with deepwater development via "unitization," a model commonly used for federally regulated drilling in the U.S. Gulf of Mexico. A framework (specifically to support unitization as a model for development, which is explained in a basic fashion in the next section) is widely recognized as necessary for offshore exploration and production to occur.

[4] For details about developments involving China, see CRS Report R42784, *Maritime Territorial and Exclusive Economic Zone (EEZ) Disputes Involving China: Issues for Congress*, by Ronald O'Rourke. For details about developments involving multinational interests in the Arctic, see CRS Report R41153, *Changes in the Arctic: Background and Issues for Congress*, coordinated by Ronald O'Rourke.

[5] Department of State, *Summary of the U.S.-Mexico Transboundary Hydrocarbons Agreement* (July 30, 2012). This summary can be found at http://www.state.gov/r/pa/prs/ps/2012/02/184235 htm.

[6] For a discussion of conditions in Mexico, see CRS Report R42917, *Mexico's Peña Nieto Administration: Priorities and Key Issues in U.S.-Mexican Relations*, by Clare Ribando Seelke.

---

Agreement. At issue is the role of Mexico's state oil company, PEMEX, specifically whether PEMEX is able to pursue deepwater operations without significant regulatory challenges.[7]

In contrast to the examination of issues underway in Mexico, the hurdle in the United States involves lack of consensus about lifting the moratorium. To date, the Bureau of Safety and Environmental Enforcement (BSEE) has not completed phasing in safety reforms promulgated by the agency in 2010 and 2011 in the wake of the *Deepwater Horizon* oil spill.[8] Without these new safety requirements (anticipated in later 2013 and 2014), there is little to counter concerns expressed by some U.S. interests dependent on water-related activities in the Gulf of Mexico (fishing, recreation, and tourism) that the moratorium is needed to prevent possible oil spill risks that can accompany deepwater drilling operations in the Gulf of Mexico.[9]

On February 20, 2012, at the signing ceremony for the Agreement, U.S. officials acknowledged that for the Agreement to take effect, both countries must review and accept it. Referring to the challenges facing the Agreement on both sides of the border, these officials praised the Agreement as a way to help both countries reach a mutual goal— improved North American energy security. Specifically, then-Secretary of State Hillary Rodham Clinton referred to "shared challenges" when announcing the Agreement: "Our actions today are further proof of how Mexico and the United States come together to solve shared challenges. From our earliest days, the Gulf of Mexico has been a source of unity for our peoples and our countries. And the steps we are taking today will help make sure it remains that way for decades to come."[10]

To date, U.S. review of the Agreement includes House and Senate passage of legislation to approve and implement the Agreement. On June 27, 2013, the House passed H.R. 1613 (H.Rept. 113-101); and on October 14, 2013, the Senate passed S. 812. Controversy surrounding House action highlighted a persistent tension between proponents of ocean oil and gas drilling seeking to accelerate production of domestic energy supplies and those who favor maintaining the moratorium in order to provide time for safety and environmental issues to be addressed.[11] The Senate passed S. 812 by unanimous consent. The legislation is discussed in greater detail below, in the section on "Pending Legislation and Related Legislative Interests."

---

[7] "Mexico's Congress Could Get Mexico Energy Reform Package Soon, Official Says," *Latin American Herald Tribune*, August 14, 2013. Full article available at http://www.laht.com/article.asp?ArticleId=812412&CategoryId=14091.

[8] Bureau of Safety and Environmental Enforcement (BSEE, pronounced "*Bessy*"), is responsible for oversight and enforcement, field operations, inspections, workforce safety, and decommissioning. For analysis of these topics as they relate to recent reforms, see CRS Report R42942, *Deepwater Horizon Oil Spill: Recent Activities and Ongoing Developments*, by Jonathan L. Ramseur and Curry L. Hagerty.

[9] For findings of the cumulative effects of multiple management changes within the DOI bureaus responsible for offshore energy production, see GAO-13-283 *High-Risk Series* (February 14, 2013). This report outlines management challenges related to drilling programs. It is updated every two years, at the start of each new Congress. See also *Department of the Interior: Major Management Challenges*, GAO-11-42T (March 1, 2011).

[10] U.S. Department of State, "Remarks by Secretary of State Hillary Rodham Clinton at the Signing of the U.S.-Mexico Transboundary Agreement," press release, February 20, 2012.

[11] The main tension expressed by supporters and opponents of H.R. 1613, as reported by the House Committee on Natural Resources, involved provisions to exempt actions taken by public companies in accordance with the transboundary hydrocarbon agreement from requirements under Section 1504 of the Dodd-Frank Act and the Securities and Exchange Commission's Natural Resource Extraction Disclosure Rule. For arguments in favor of these provisions, see H.Rept. 113-101, and for counterarguments, see "Statement of Administration Policy on H.R. 1613" (June 25, 2013), at http://www.whitehouse.gov/sites/default/files/omb/legislative/sap/113/saphr1613r_20130625.pdf.

Congress can act on the Agreement throughout the remainder of the 113th Congress, or can defer action indefinitely. While the Agreement awaits U.S. attention, the moratorium that was established in a previous treaty remains in effect until 2014, or until another acceptable alternative (diplomatic or legislative) supersedes it.

## Recent Developments

Proposed legislation providing the Secretary of the Interior the authority to implement the Transboundary Agreement has passed in both chambers: (S. 812 passed in the Senate; H.R. 1613 passed in the House). Lawmakers favoring these bills express support for a goal found in both bills—providing congressional approval of the Agreement. Objections to the legislation were expressed by those in Congress opposed to provisions found only in H.R. 1613, as reported by the House Committee on Natural Resources. These provisions would exempt actions taken by public companies from requirements under a section of the Securities and Exchange Commission's Natural Resource Extraction Disclosure Rule. It is widely recognized that, among other provisions found in H.R. 1613, those clarifying this disclosure requirement involve issues beyond implementing the Agreement.

In both chambers, supporters and opponents have expressed an increased interest in legislation to achieve goals limited to approving and implementing the Agreement to establish a framework for the cooperative exploration and development of oil and gas reservoirs that cross the international maritime boundary in the Gulf of Mexico. While opponents express specific objections to certain provisions aimed at other objectives (found in H.R. 1613,[12] but not in S. 812), committee chairs and ranking members in both chambers have pledged expeditious approval of proposed implementing legislation. Legislative action is discussed in greater detail below.

## Policy Review: U.S. Offshore Oil and Gas Leasing System

In its current form, the federally regulated offshore oil and gas leasing system comprises roughly 1.7 billion acres beyond state waters, including the U.S. exclusive economic zone (EEZ) and areas beyond the U.S. EEZ.[13] Responsibility for managing ocean energy resources falls within the U.S. Department of State and the U.S. Department of the Interior's (DOI's) Bureau of Ocean Energy Management (BOEM).[14] Conveying U.S. leases through lease sales and managing the leasing system (from early planning to decommissioning) is achieved mainly through the Five-Year Outer Continental Shelf Oil and Gas Leasing Program[15] and the Offshore Renewable Energy

---

[12] As noted in the Statement of Administration Policy on H.R. 1613, the Administration supports implementing legislation, without the inclusion of provisions such as those relating to Section 1504 of the Dodd-Frank Act that arguably would dilute U.S. efforts to increase transparency and accountability.

[13] The U.S. EEZ generally includes territory 200 nautical miles seaward of state waters. See Presidential Proclamation No. 5030, 48 *Federal Register* 10605 (March 14, 1983).

[14] Bureau of Ocean Energy Management (BOEM, rhymes with "*Rome*") is tasked with offshore leasing administration, including developing maps, completing scientific and economic analyses, and issuing leases. BOEM also participates in some international relations missions regarding U.S. ocean energy resources.

[15] See Five-Year OCS Oil and Gas Leasing Program 2012-2017. This program was approved on August 27, 2012, and is anticipated to be in place through 2017. Each program is mandated by the Outer Continental Shelf Lands Act (43 U.S.C. §1344) to be "a schedule of proposed lease sales indicating, as precisely as possible, the size, timing, and location of leasing activity which ... will best meet national energy needs."

Program.[16] Consistent with the objectives of each program, BOEM manages more than 8,000 active leases organized in a grid system that was established at the start of the program in 1953.[17]

U.S. ocean energy production currently accounts for 26% of domestic oil production and about 16% of domestic natural gas production. While most offshore acreage is found in the Alaska region (approximately 1.03 billion acres of a total of 1.7 billion acres), oil and gas leases are located mainly in the Gulf of Mexico (89% of the federally regulated offshore energy activity is concentrated in an area accounting for about 2% of U.S. waters). **Figure 1** illustrates generally where U.S. oil and gas lease sales take place in the Gulf of Mexico.

Specifically, **Figure 1** depicts ocean areas in the Gulf of Mexico in relation to coastal states and cities, highlighting areas eligible for lease sales (shaded areas) and areas ineligible for lease sales (unshaded areas).[18] In addition to generating domestic energy supplies in these areas, federally regulated offshore energy projects are recognized as generating significant public receipts, including approximately $6.9 billion in 2012.[19] U.S. lease sales in the Gulf of Mexico resulted in reported revenues totaling over $13 billion in the last two years.[20] DOI estimates future revenues of $50 million in 2014 from energy activities projected to take place in the transboundary area if the Agreement is accepted and implemented.[21]

---

[16] 43 U.S.C. §1337(p). For more information about deployment of renewable energy projects, see http://www.boem.gov/Renewable-Energy-Program/Smart-from-the-Start/Index.aspx.

[17] After 1953 the federal land tenure system reflected a federal grid system beginning seaward of state submerged land tenure systems. Starting in1983 this grid system recognized the U.S. EEZ.

[18] For the purposes of this report, the state and federal waters of the Gulf of Mexico are defined as follows: Florida waters extend 9 nautical miles (10.4 statute miles) from shore; Louisiana, Mississippi, and Alabama state waters extend 3 nautical miles (or 3.5 statute miles) from shore; and Texas state waters extend 9 nautical miles (10.4 statute miles) from shore. For a comprehensive analysis of coastal and marine uses in the western Gulf of Mexico, see *2012-2017 Western Planning Area/Central Planning Area Multisale Environmental Impact Statement (EIS),* BOEM, available at http://www.boem.gov/uploadedFiles/BOEM/Environmental_Stewardship/Environmental_Assessment/NEPA/BOEM-2012-019_v3.pdf.

[19] Statistics about annual energy supplies and annual receipts from bonus bids, rentals, and royalties are published through numerous sources. The statistics in this report are derived from the Office of Natural Resources Revenue within DOI, available at http://www.ONRR.gov.

[20] For ocean energy revenue statistics, see http://www.ONRR.gov. FY2012 federal offshore reported revenues were $6.9 billion; FY2011, $6.5 billion; and FY2010, $5.3 billion.

[21] See DOI *FY2014 Congressional Budget Justification,* Bureau of Ocean Energy Management (BOEM), p. 12. DOI bases this statement on assumptions about bonus payments and other predicted revenue streams for rentals and taxes deriving from operations in the transboundary area cited in the Agreement. Estimates of federal budget effects vary widely. For example, a recent estimate by the Congressional Budget Office (CBO) provided as part of analysis of a specific bill to implement the Agreement (H.R. 1613) concluded that approving and implementing the Agreement in that instance would increase federal receipts by $25 million from 2014 through 2023.

**Figure 1. U.S. Gulf of Mexico in Relation to Selected Coastal States and Cities**

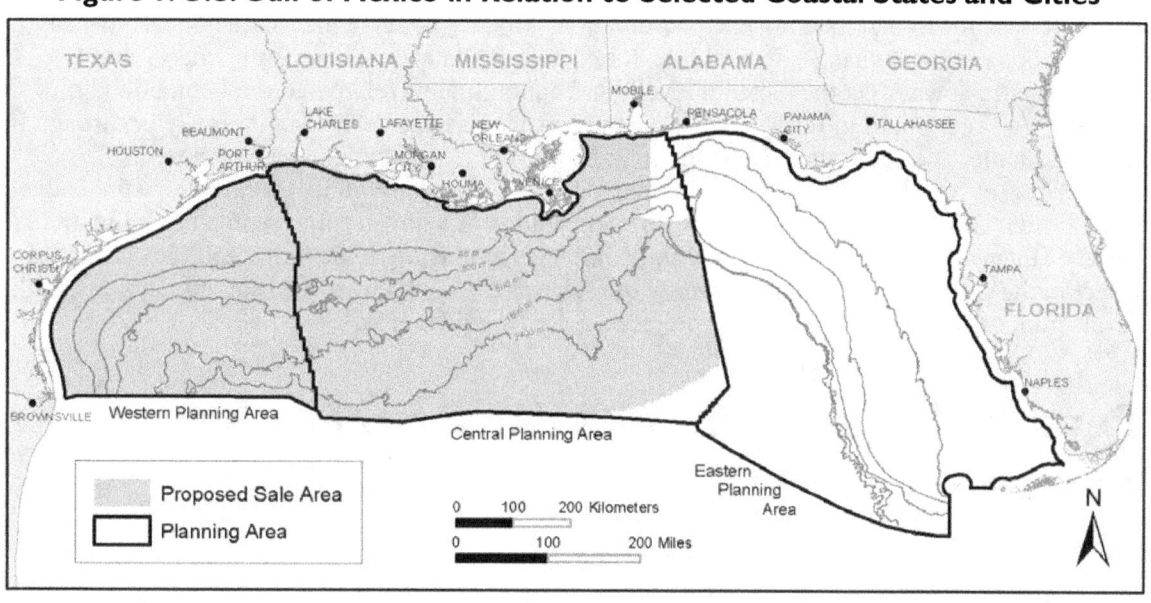

**Source:** BOEM.

National ownership and use of ocean resources are issues attracting increased attention in Congress, particularly when they involve transboundary areas of international waters.[22] Competing national interests in offshore drilling stir questions: How does Congress balance the nation's interests in resource use and protection in international ocean areas? What are effective ways to monitor safety at international marine borders, particularly when the marine areas fall under the jurisdiction of multiple federal agencies?[23] Some in Congress have expressed an interest in these questions through legislative proposals, program oversight, and annual appropriations for the relevant federal agencies.

## U.S.-Mexico Transboundary Hydrocarbons Agreement

The Agreement is widely recognized as an initial step toward a joint development scenario involving three U.S.-Mexico commitments: (1) eliminating the moratorium in waters beyond their respective exclusive economic zones (EEZs); (2) studying the transboundary areas (exchanging geological information); and (3) potentially deploying joint oil and gas operations associated with developing transboundary reservoirs.[24]

---

[22] International customary law provides frameworks for governance of some but not all areas and activities beyond national jurisdictions such as a nation's EEZ. One widely recognized framework is the United Nations Convention of the Law of the Sea (UNCLOS), a multilateral treaty with which the United States participates as a non-party. While not directly applicable to U.S-Mexico bilateral compacts in the Gulf of Mexico, Article 76 of UNCLOS has provided a process for claiming extended continental shelf (ECS) areas resulting in territorial claims reaching 350 nautical miles from a country's coastal areas.

[23] Each of these issues is discussed in the section of this report entitled "Pending Legislation."

[24] Joint commitments listed in the Agreement involve goals for the safe and equitable exploitation of transboundary reservoirs. These commitments are intended to unfold over many years through further negotiations aimed at facilitating more specific approaches to such issues as standards for operations and environmental review. Until the Agreement is accepted, the timeline for implementation remains unclear. Numerous federal regulators might be involved in activities covered by the Agreement. Operational safety and revenue obligations related to any future oil (continued...)

---

Under the current statutory framework, U.S. commitments fall into three basic categories: commitments relative to federal-state coordination[25] (mainly to recognize state policies in state waters); commitments that are federal in nature[26] (mainly balancing competing energy and environmental interests at the national level); and commitments relative to the international context[27] (a fluid mix of military, trade, and diplomatic missions derived unilaterally or through nation-to-nation mechanisms). Given the fragmented and overlapping nature of these three categories, several questions have arisen related to how U.S. commitments under the Agreement might affect U.S. interests. Would the Agreement lead to any new legal or regulatory obligations for U.S. interests? Would existing environmental laws or existing lease terms and conditions in effect in the Gulf of Mexico be affected by the Agreement? What, if any, fiscal implications might result from carrying out collaborative projects in the boundary area?

# Pending Legislation and Related Legislative Interests

The Administration and some in and outside of Congress have advocated for swift U.S. review and acceptance of the Agreement. Others have expressed skepticism that the Agreement is an optimal approach to expand the ocean energy portfolio in the Gulf of Mexico. Two legislative initiatives (H.R. 1613 and S. 812) were introduced as part of the U.S. review of the Agreement. Each bill would accept the Agreement, taking a slightly different approach to implementation.

## H.R. 1613

H.R. 1613, "Outer Continental Shelf Transboundary Hydrocarbon Agreements Authorization Act," was considered and passed by the House on June 27, 2013.[28] This legislation would establish guidelines and procedures for implementing the Agreement; and among other measures,

---

(...continued)
and gas leases have already been delegated to BOEM. See CRS Report R42599, *Department of the Interior (DOI) Reorganization of Ocean Energy Programs*, by Curry L. Hagerty.

[25] The Submerged Lands Act (SLA), 43 U.S.C. §§1301 et seq. Consistent with SLA, most federal obligations are defined relative to the jurisdictional bounds of state and federal waters.

[26] The Outer Continental Shelf Lands Act of 1953 (OCSLA), 43 U.S.C. §§1331 et seq. Consistent with OCSLA, federal mandatory and discretionary responsibilities are defined for energy resource management and revenue management in areas beyond state waters referred to as the Outer Continental Shelf (OCS).

[27] U.S. commitments relative to managing ocean energy resources in international waters involve various treaties. Separate from the U.S.-Mexico bilateral treaties discussed above, the United States is party to four prominent ocean governance treaties adopted in 1958: Convention on the Territorial Sea and the Contiguous Zone, Convention on the High Seas, Convention on the Continental Shelf, and Convention on Fishing and Conservation of the Living Resources of the High Seas.

[28] To help understand the role of the House of Representatives with respect to review of this Agreement, it is important to clarify that the Agreement has not been submitted to the Senate as a treaty. Under the U.S. system, a legally binding international agreement can take different forms. Unlike agreements taking the form of a treaty (that would enter into force if approved by a two-thirds majority of the Senate and subsequently ratified by the President), this Agreement was negotiated and signed by the executive branch as a non-treaty. In the case of a non-treaty, to be legally binding, it must either be authorized by a statute passed by Congress ("congressional executive agreements") or a prior treaty approved by the Senate, except when it concerns matters falling under the exclusive constitutional authority of the President ("sole executive agreements"). For further discussion, see CRS Report RL32528, *International Law and Agreements: Their Effect upon U.S. Law*, by Michael John Garcia.

---

would provide for legislative review of any future agreements governing that area. The bill would amend the Outer Continental Shelf Lands Act (OCSLA, 43 U.S.C. 1331 et seq.) to implement the Agreement by providing new powers to the Secretary of the Interior for approving unitization agreements.[29]

By adding a new section to the end of the OCSLA ("Section 32"), the bill authorizes the Secretary to implement the Agreement with Mexico by completing the following steps:

- submitting the Agreement to the Speaker of the House; the Majority Leader of the Senate; the Chairs of the House Committee on Natural Resources and the Senate Committee on Energy and Natural Resources;

- including in the submission (1) legislation relevant to implementation; (2) economic analysis of impacts of the Agreement on domestic production of offshore oil and gas resources; (3) a description of regulations expected to be issued to implement the Agreement; and (4) provisions adopting unitization as the approach to developing the area.[30]

Furthermore, H.R. 1613 would exempt U.S. firms from certain reporting requirements of the Securities Exchange Act of 1934.[31] Currently, publicly traded companies are required to disclose certain information regarding business dealings related to extractive operations to investors through filings with the Securities and Exchange Commission (SEC). Section 1504 of the Dodd-Frank Wall Street Reform and Consumer Protection Act of 2010 (P.L. 111-203) amended the Securities Exchange Act of 1934 by expanding certain required public company disclosures.[32] When applied to the commercial development of oil, natural gas, or minerals, the act requires the disclosure of certain payments made to the federal government or foreign governments by public companies required to file annual reports with the SEC. The provision in H.R. 1613 entitled "Exemption from Resources Extraction" provides that actions taken by such a public company pertaining to any transboundary hydrocarbon agreement shall be exempt from such disclosure requirements.[33]

## S. 812[34]

This bill would authorize the Secretary of the Interior to implement the Agreement in a manner consistent with legislative provisions proposed by the Administration and referred to in the

---

[29] H.R. 1613 was referred to three committees: Committee on Natural Resources; Committee on Foreign Affairs and Committee on Financial Services. On June 6, 2013, the Committees on Foreign Affairs and Financial Services discharged the bill.

[30] In addition, H.R. 1613 offers placeholders for implementing Agreements with four other countries: Canada, Russia, the Bahamas, and Bermuda. Although placeholders are sometimes included in bills that are introduced, they have rarely been enacted as law.

[31] Securities Exchange Act of 1934, 157 U.S.C. 78m(q).This section of the bill is summarized by Gary Shorter, CRS Specialist in Financial Economics.

[32] CRS Report R41350, *The Dodd-Frank Wall Street Reform and Consumer Protection Act: Issues and Summary*, coordinated by Baird Webel.

[33] In general, the American Petroleum Institute (API) and other business groups have resisted implementation of Section 1504 of the Dodd-Frank Act. This resistance has been demonstrated by challenging SEC's new rule requiring publicly traded U.S. oil and gas companies to report information about projects that potentially could benefit their overseas national oil companies.

[34] Descriptions of SEC obligations were authored by Gary Shorter, CRS Specialist in Financial Economics.

Administration's 2014 budget request.[35] Specifically, under the legislative proposal referred to in the budget request and under S. 812, the Secretary of the Interior is provided with new authorities to approve unitization agreements and related arrangements within certain guidelines. This approach contrasts with H.R. 1613 in several respects.

A key distinction between the Senate and House bills is the additional provisions in the House bill, particularly regarding disclosure requirements for investment information pursuant to U.S. Securities and Exchange Commission (SEC) rules. Specifically, the House bill clarifies the application of Section 13(q) of the Securities Exchange Act of 1934[36] in matters related to joint development projects in the transboundary area. In contrast, S. 812 is silent on this point, not addressing the treatment of U.S. firms and SEC obligations.

## Related Legislative Interests

Congressional interests relevant to U.S. legislative implementation of this Agreement include the following:

- **Hearings Addressing a Range of Public Lands Issues.** Multiple oversight hearings in the House and Senate during the 113th Congress have involved lawmakers examining how current federal resource management laws govern energy production. These hearings reflect two visions: seeing the need to grant access to some areas to enhance energy production and —as a counterbalance— seeing the need to defer access to some areas to protect people and the environment from risk. As part of hearings about offshore energy development, some Members are proposing statutory changes related to the following: (1) alternatives to current programs for allocating federal receipts generated from drilling operations and offshore wind farms; (2) deployment of more diverse ocean energy technologies in a wider range of locations; and (3) changes in the pace of inspections and permitting. To date, legislative attention to these various themes demonstrates that lawmakers are considering statutory changes by addressing the U.S. offshore energy program as a whole. In contrast to piecemeal approaches of the past, there seems to be an interest in examining a broad agenda of interlocking issues to achieve a more diverse U.S. portfolio in the Gulf of Mexico and beyond.

---

[35] See DOI FY2014 Budget Justifications, "Budget Highlights," p. 23. See also BOEM Office of Congressional Affairs written communication to CRS, May 16, 2013. The budget justification refers to draft legislation offered by the Administration to the House and the Senate as follows:

> The Secretary is authorized to take actions necessary to implement the terms of the Agreement between the United States of America and the United Mexican States Concerning Transboundary Hydrocarbon Reservoirs in the Gulf of Mexico, which is hereby approved, including: to approve unitization agreements and related arrangements for the exploration of, and development or production of oil or gas from, transboundary reservoirs and geological structures; to disclose as necessary under such an Agreement information related to the exploration, development, and production of a transboundary reservoir or geological structure that may be considered confidential, privileged, or proprietary information under law; and to accept and take action not inconsistent with an expert determination under such an Agreement.

[36] 157 U.S.C. 78m(q). For a discussion of this theme, see http://thehill.com/blogs/e2-wire/e2-wire/296235-house-gop-moves-to-shield-oil-companies-from-disclosure-rules#ixzz2RyR0jqGZ.

---

## What, If Anything, Has Changed Since the Gulf Oil Spill of 2010?

In the aftermath of the April 20, 2010, explosion and fire on the *Deepwater Horizon*[37] in the Gulf of Mexico, federal regulators reexamined some of the risks and benefits accompanying deepwater drilling, bolstered enforcement measures related to operational safety, and revised standards for certain deepwater drilling operations.

Perceptions about the adequacy of these federal reforms vary. As implementation of these reforms continues to unfold, some in Congress have expressed an interest in how the reforms might be affecting energy production, worker safety, and environmental protection in U.S. waters.[38]

More than one Government Accountability Office (GAO) study is underway to offer insights on DOI agency performance as part of a broader look at how federal offshore areas are managed.[39]

---

- **Regulatory Actions to Solicit Bids for Ocean Tracts in the Transboundary Area.** As part of periodically conducting U.S. lease sales to convey development rights in ocean tracts in the Gulf of Mexico, BOEM has offered leases for oil and gas development rights pursuant to treaty terms established in 2000. As in the past, BOEM has announced that any bids on the transboundary area would not be opened until after both parties have accepted the Agreement. Specifically, as part of offering offshore oil and gas development rights beyond the U.S. EEZ and near the marine boundary area with Mexico, in 2012 BOEM conducted Sale 229,[40] and in 2013, Sale 233.[41] Agency preparation for these lease sales has included offering maps of offshore areas depicting where the U.S. grid is located with respect to leased and unleased tracts and stipulating certain lease terms and conditions related to tracts in the transboundary area.

- **Diplomatic Cooperation on Oil Spill Risks.** For decades, U.S.-Mexico cooperation on oil spill risks has included planning strategies to cope with

---

[37] The *Deepwater Horizon* events resulted in 11 worker fatalities, a massive oil release, and a national response effort in the Gulf of Mexico led by the federal government. Based on estimates from the U.S. Geological Survey, the oil spill was the largest in U.S. waters.

[38] 76 *Federal Register* 64432 (October 18, 2011). BSEE revised 30 CFR Chapter II. For a status report, see CRS Report R42942, *Deepwater Horizon Oil Spill: Recent Activities and Ongoing Developments*, by Jonathan L. Ramseur and Curry L. Hagerty.

[39] Gene L. Dodaro, U.S. Comptroller General, testimony before the House Committee on Oversight and Government Reform, February 17, 2011; Committee on Appropriations, Subcommittee on Interior, Hearing March 17, 2011. GAO-13-283 *High-Risk Series* (February 14, 2013). This GAO report is updated at the start of each new Congress.

[40] On November 28, 2012, BOEM offered offshore oil and gas development rights beyond the U.S. EEZ and near the marine boundary area with Mexico as part of the public lease sale referred to as Sale 229. Prior to U.S. leasing activities near the U.S.-Mexico continental shelf boundary, BOEM issued the following statement: "Within 30 days following the approval of the Agreement between the United States of America and the United Mexican States Concerning Transboundary Hydrocarbon Reservoirs in the Gulf of Mexico or by May 31, 2013, whichever occurs first, the Secretary of the Interior will determine whether it is in the best interest of the United States either to open bids for boundary area blocks or to return the bids unopened." The sale drew 131 bids on 116 ocean tracts from 13 companies. Ocean tracts offered at the sale were located from just beyond Texas state waters to acreage beyond the U.S. EEZ. A previous Western Gulf lease sale (Sale 218 conducted in December 2011) offered acreage in this general area, attracting 241 bids on 191 ocean tracts from 20 companies. For details about the most recent sale, see http://www.boem.gov/Oil-and-Gas-Energy-Program/Leasing/Regional-Leasing/Gulf-of-Mexico-Region/Lease-Sales/229/index.aspx.

[41] This sale entailed 3,864 tracts from 9 to more than 250 miles off the U.S. coast, in water depths ranging from 16 to more than 10,975 feet. BOEM estimated this lease sale could result in the production of 116 million to 200 million barrels of oil and 538 billion to 938 billion cubic feet of natural gas. Following this sale, bids are going through an evaluation process within BOEM to ensure the public receives fair market value before a lease is awarded. Sale statistics for Sale 233 can be found at http://www.boem.gov/Sale-233.

---

pollution caused by oil spills. Both countries participate regularly in a joint contingency planning in order to ensure adequate response to spills.[42] The current joint plan—known as Mexus Plan—sets standard operating procedures in case of incidents that threaten the coastal waters or marine environment of the border zone of both countries. The U.S. response team is coordinated by the Coast Guard's Assistant Commandant for Marine Safety and Environmental Protection.[43]

# Relevant Geographic Areas

The Agreement reflects a continued commitment by the United States and Mexico to identify and define certain geographic areas located beyond each country's EEZ. These areas were first recognized by both countries through diplomatic channels in 1978. **Figure 2** illustrates these areas in relation to U.S.-Mexico treaty lines.[44]

The recognition by the United States and Mexico of certain geographic areas located beyond each country's EEZ is consistent with customary international law relevant to countries planning to regulate drilling operations beyond their EEZs. Areas beyond the U.S.-Mexico EEZs are largely unexamined for oil and gas development. As a result, there is not a robust collection of data about impacts of energy development on particular populations and ecosystems. Both countries' diplomats have stated plans to monitor activities taking place in transboundary areas as a component of a joint development scenario.

The line-striped areas depicted in **Figure 2** illustrate areas defined by treaty. These areas are sometimes referred to as "gaps" (specifically the "Western Gap" and the "Eastern Gap"). This signifies not only a gap that exists in how nations define the legal status of that area, but also a gap in available scientific information about the area.

---

[42] U.S. Department of State, "Mexico, Pollution: Marine Environment, Agreement signed July 24, 1980," TIAS, 10021.

[43] U.S. Coast Guard, "Mexus Plan, The Joint Contingency Plan Between the United Mexican States and the United States of America Regarding Pollution of the Marine Environment by Discharges of Hydrocarbons and Other Hazardous Substance," February 25, 2000. Furthermore, *National Commission on the BP Deepwater Horizon Oil Spill and Offshore Drilling* January 2011, reports that Mexico already conducts safety drills in the Gulf of Mexico and that it is in the U.S. national interest to engage in a common, rigorous system of regulatory oversight to cooperate on containment and response strategies in case of a spill. See *Deepwater, The Gulf Oil Disaster and the Future of Offshore Drilling,* Report to the President, p. 254 and p. 300, at http://www.oilspillcommission.gov/sites/default/files/documents/DEEPWATER_ReporttothePresident_FINAL.pdf.

[44] In these areas, referred to as "gaps," national marine boundaries have not been fully defined. The Western Gap is the polygon located near the Mexican coast of Tamaulipas and the U.S. coast of Houston, TX. The Eastern Gap is the polygon located near the Mexican coast of Yucatan, the U.S. coast of New Orleans, LA, and the coast of Cuba. A discussion of the Eastern Gap is beyond the scope of this report. The Western Gap is depicted in **Figure 6**.

---

**Figure 2. Basic Features of the Western and Eastern Gaps in the Gulf of Mexico**

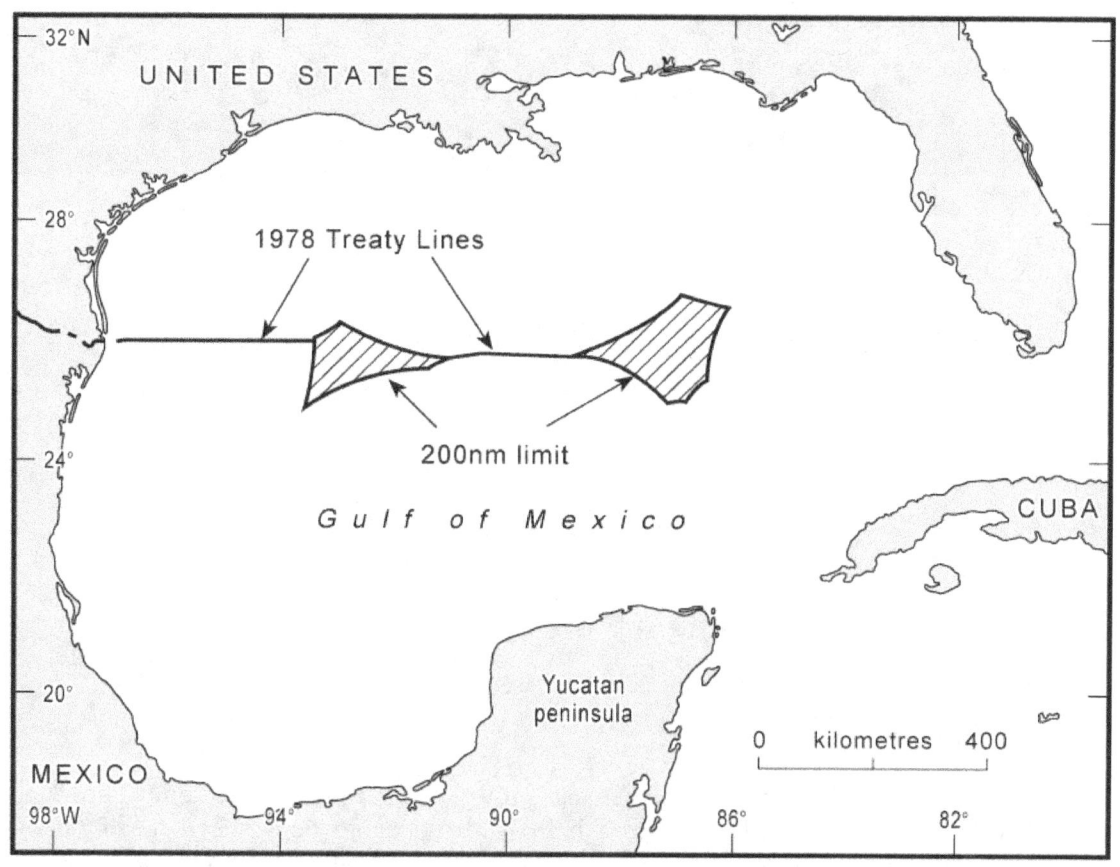

**Source:** Adapted by CRS from International Boundaries Research Unit (IBRU) 1997. Line-striped areas are the western and eastern polygons representing "gaps" where national marine boundaries have not been fully defined.

## Western Gap

The Western Gap is the polygon located in **Figure 2** in the western portion of the Gulf of Mexico and in **Figure 3** as the main image. The Western Gap encompasses about 4.2 million acres. Although the Western Gap falls outside both the U.S. and Mexico EEZs, most of the acreage is recognized as belonging to either the United States or Mexico, while a certain portion falls along the transboundary line between U.S. and Mexican waters. The U.S. acreage in the Western Gap includes about 1.5 million acres to the north of the transboundary area.[45] Of the U.S. acreage within the Western Gap, the portion falling in the transboundary area and covered by the moratorium measures 158,584 acres. Some ocean acreage in the U.S. portion of the Western Gap (other than the transboundary area covered by moratorium) has been offered at U.S. lease sales since 2001.[46]

---

[45] According to BOEM, the division of the Western Gap allocates 1,507,840 acres or 38% to the United States and 2,624,000 acres or 62% to Mexico.

[46] See H.Rept. 113-101, Part 1, p. 4. "Currently, there are 67 active lease blocks held by nine companies on the U.S. portion of the Western Gap, meaning roughly 20% of the available acreage in the Western Gap area is under lease." For a discussion of U.S. leasing activities in the western Gulf of Mexico beyond the U.S. EEZ and potentially subject to the (continued...)

**Figure 3. Detail of Western Gap in the Gulf of Mexico Showing U.S. and Mexico EEZ**

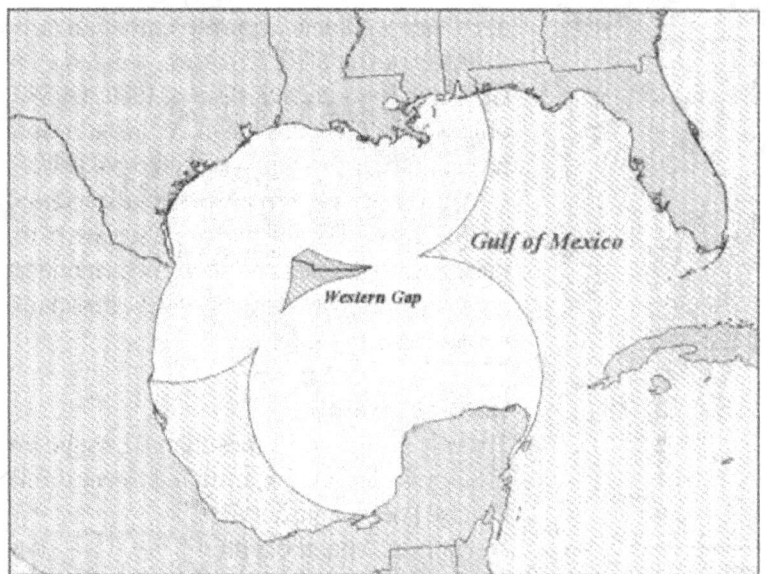

**Source:** CRS modifications to image available from National Geodetic Survey (NGS) National Ocean Service (NOS) National Oceanic and Atmospheric Administration (NOAA) at http://www.ngs.noaa.gov/CORS/Articles/solgps.pdf.

## Transboundary Area

The transboundary area defined in the Agreement is illustrated in **Figure 4** as a solid yellow line running east beyond Texas state waters, through the Western Gap, to the western edge of the Eastern Gap. As discussed above, the U.S. portion of this area encompasses 1.5 million acres, located in a corridor also referred to as the Delimitation Line.

---

(...continued)

provisions of international agreements, see *U.S. Accession to U.N. Convention on the Law of the Sea Unnecessary to Develop Oil and Gas Resources, Backgrounder No. 2668*, by Steven Groves, May 14, 2012, p. 9.

**Figure 4. Delimitation Line Defined by the Agreement**

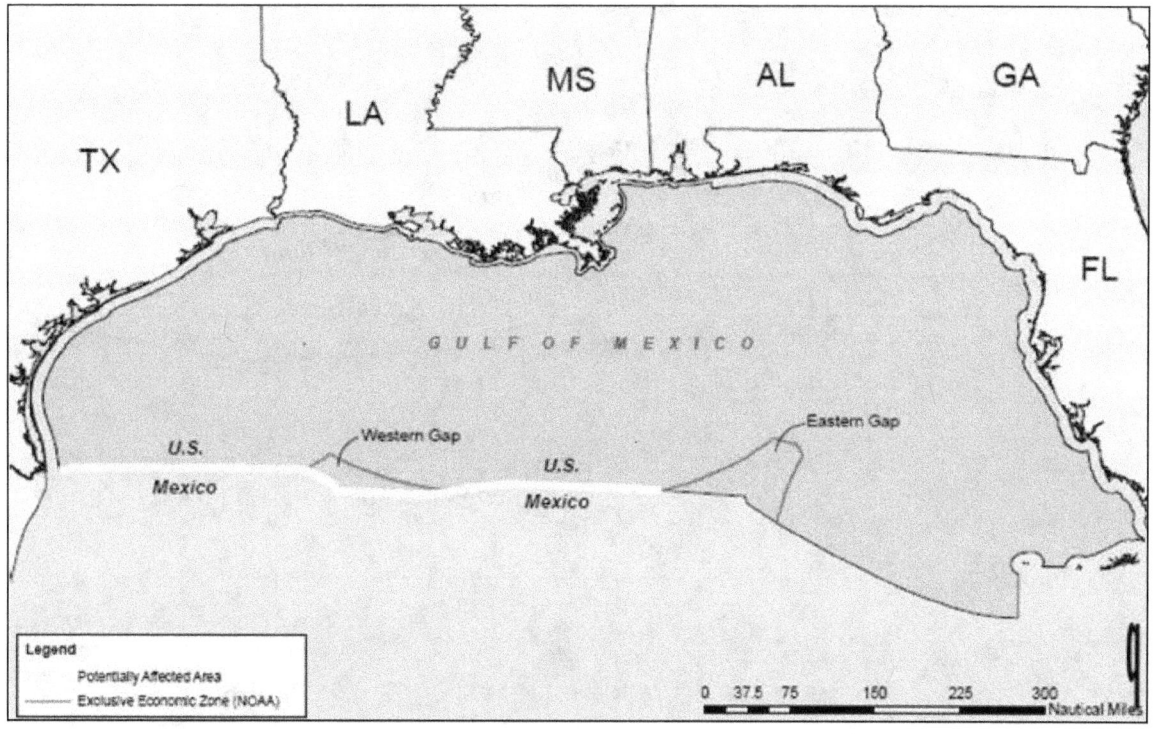

**Source:** BOEM. U.S. side of the Western Gap (1.5 million U.S. acres) and the Eastern Gap (undetermined U.S. acreage) is shown. Mexican coastal areas are not shown.

## Moratorium Area

The moratorium area is located entirely inside the Western Gap, along the transboundary line. It comprises a narrow (2.8 nautical miles) corridor cutting across a 135-mile distance (158,584 acres).[47] The moratorium area attracts attention, partly because, as **Figure 5** illustrates, it is located in a mid-section of the 550-mile transboundary area.

Consistent with U.S.-Mexico treaty provisions, this moratorium expires in 2014. In the absence of applicable measures to the contrary, and absent clearance to lift the ban pursuant to the Agreement, the following actions are possible: allowing the moratorium to expire without further indication of international relations relative to managing the area; extending the moratorium for an agreeable time frame; or replacing the moratorium with some other alternative to which the United States and Mexico may need to agree.

---

[47] Analysis of the Eastern Gap area is beyond the scope of this report. For more information about the Eastern Gap and how the U.S.-Mexican boundaries for this area were drawn, see *GPS World* (May, 2001) available at http://www.ngs noaa.gov/CORS/Articles/solgps.pdf.

**Figure 5. Illustration of the Moratorium Area Located in the Western Gap**

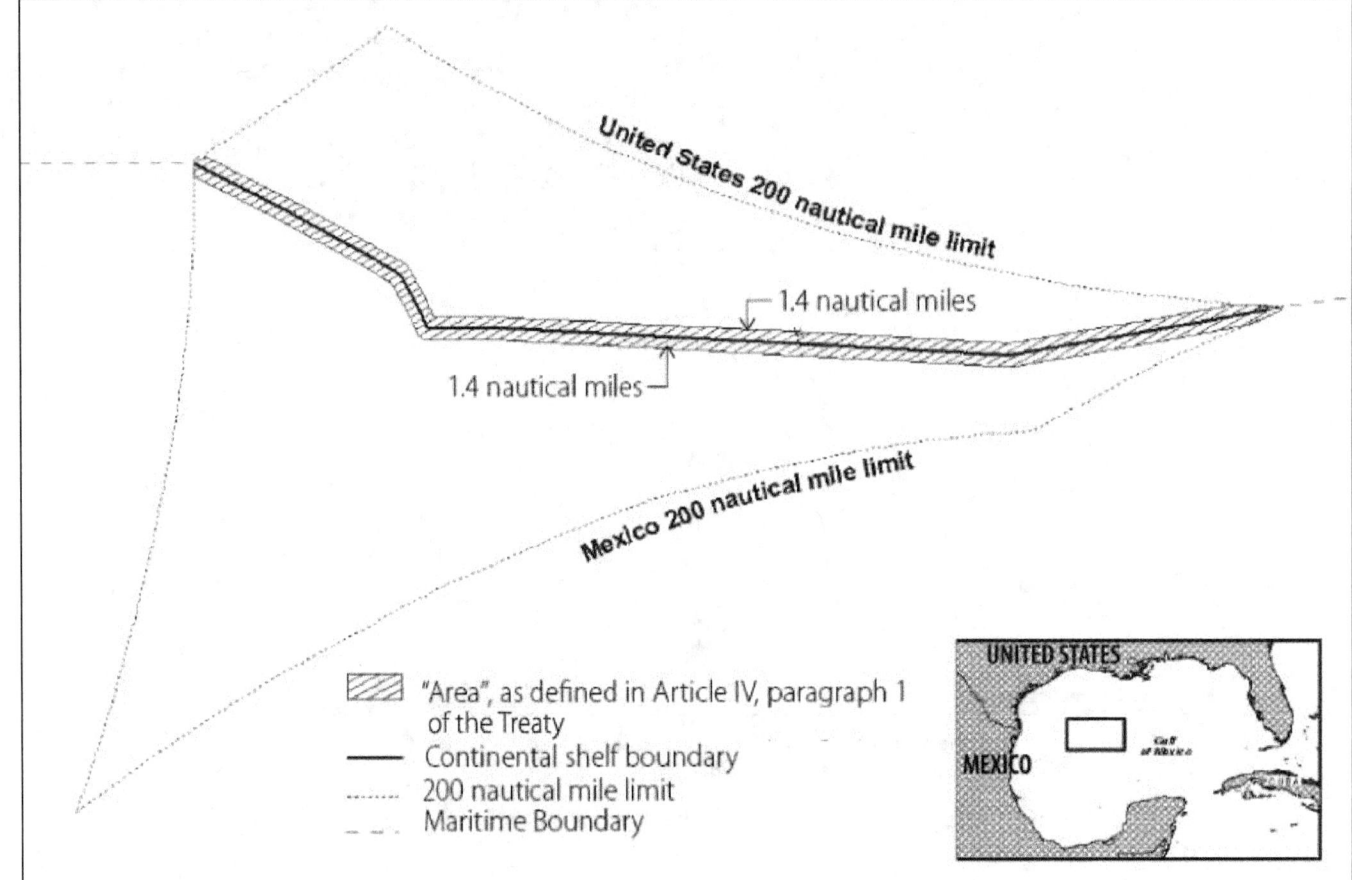

**Source:** CRS, adapted from the treaty documents submitted by U.S. negotiators in support of *Treaty between the Government of the United Mexican States and the Government of the United States of America on the Continental Shelf* signed on June 9, 2000.

Upon signing the Agreement, U.S. negotiators elaborated on various diplomatic activities, including plans to eliminate the moratorium after review and acceptance of the Agreement by both countries.[48] Further commitments included providing U.S. leaseholders with a framework for exploiting transboundary reservoirs through "unitization";[49] encouraging options for investment; offering predictable resolution of disputes; and ensuring a joint safety regime.[50] These commitments spark a tension between the perceived need to commence oil and gas operations and the notion that deferring such operations through the moratorium would provide

---

[48] U.S. Department of State, *Summary of the U.S.–Mexico Transboundary Hydrocarbons Agreement*, July 30, 2012, http://www.state.gov/r/pa/prs/ps/2012/02/184235 htm. For the purpose of this report, all treaties are referred to by the year the treaty is signed. Accordingly, this treaty is the "1970 Treaty." In November 1970, the two nations established their maritime boundaries in the Gulf of Mexico; the treaty entered into force on April 18, 1972.

[49] Transboundary reservoirs straddle marine areas between government (nations or U.S. coastal states). Unitization is one approach to determining the recovery of oil from these areas. This concept is discussed throughout this report and is defined in the text box on p. 19.

[50] For the full set of remarks at the signing of the U.S.-Mexico Transboundary Agreement, Los Cabos, Mexico, February 20, 2012, see http://www.state.gov/secretary/rm/2012/02/184236 htm.

more time to resolve domestic regulatory policy dilemmas. This tension is discussed in the section "Issues for Congress."

## Figure 6. Selected Features of the Transboundary Area

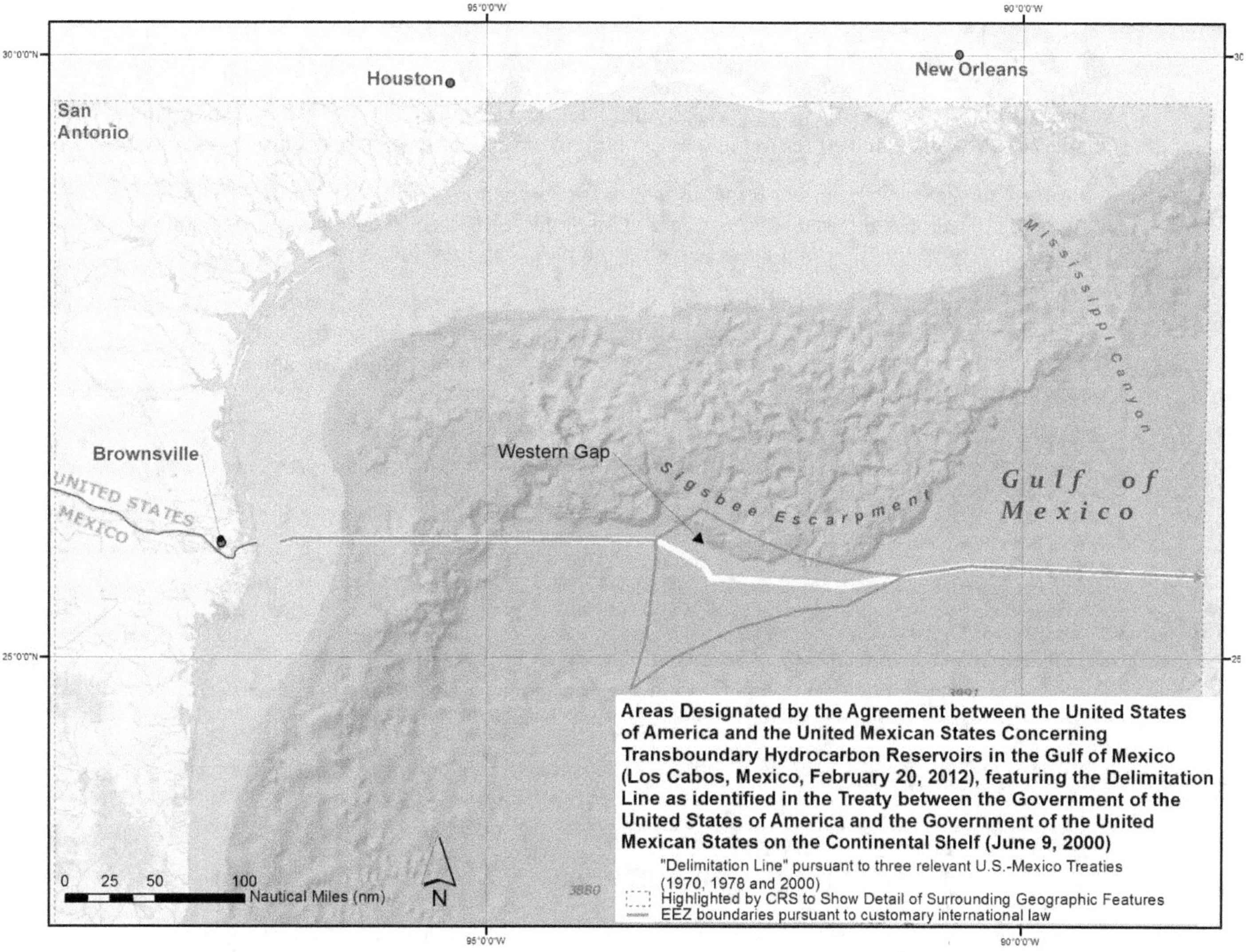

**Source:** CRS.

**Notes:** CRS designed this image to feature lines detailed in the Agreement. Specifically, CRS used point data from the Treaty between the Government of the United States of America and the Government of the United Mexican States on the Delimitation of the Continental Shelf in the Western Gulf of Mexico beyond 200 Nautical Miles, June 9, 2000. This image also features locations of the Sigsbee Escarpment and the Mississippi Canyon, not detailed in the Treaty or depicted in other images in this report.

# Concise Summary of the Agreement[51]

This section introduces readers to the contents of the Agreement by summarizing some major concepts found in all seven chapters and 27 articles. Provisions attracting particular attention include Chapter 3 (Articles 10-13: establishing a joint development scenario) and Chapter 7 (Article 24: terminating the current moratorium).

**Chapter 1** (Articles 1-5) describes the "General Principles" of the Agreement including the scope,[52] definitions,[53] jurisdiction[54] and activities near the Delimitation Line.[55] Furthermore, this chapter establishes a process for jointly determining the existence of transboundary reservoirs.[56]

**Chapter 2** (Articles 6-9) outlines joint guidelines for companies from both countries to jointly explore and develop transboundary resources cited in the Agreement. These guidelines entail a "Unitization Agreement;"[57] joint management principles;[58] and production allocations.[59]

**Chapter 3** (Articles 10-13) establishes requirements related to agreements involving unit operators.[60] It states broad guidelines addressing commercial aspects of the following: operations subject to a unit operation agreement[61] and fiscal terms related to exploiting oil and natural gas reservoirs in specific areas.[62]

---

[51] This section does not provide a comprehensive legal examination of the Agreement's contents and does not offer an in-depth analysis of U.S. interests in various provisions. A variety of topics addressed in other CRS reports analyze policy perspectives surrounding U.S. interests in the Agreement: peacetime military engagement; fisheries enforcement, search and rescue, drug interdiction, trade, investment and marine pollution law enforcement. These topics are distinct in many ways from topics surrounding U.S. interests in managing ocean energy resources in U.S. waters. For more information on these aspects of U.S.-Mexico relations, see CRS Report R42917, *Mexico's Peña Nieto Administration: Priorities and Key Issues in U.S.-Mexican Relations*, by Clare Ribando Seelke; CRS Report R41349, *U.S.-Mexican Security Cooperation: The Mérida Initiative and Beyond*, by Clare Ribando Seelke and Kristin Finklea; and CRS Report R42965, *NAFTA at 20: Overview and Trade Effects*, by M. Angeles Villarreal and Ian F. Fergusson.

[52] Article 1 provides that the Agreement applies to areas extending "across the Delimitation Line" This line begins beyond 9 nautical miles from the coastline of Texas and ends 550 miles to the east, at the point to the west of the Eastern Gap.

[53] Article 2 provides definitions for 24 terms, starting with "Confidential Data" and ending with "Unit Operating Agreement."

[54] Article 3 states that nothing in the Agreement "shall be interpreted as affecting the sovereign rights and the jurisdiction which each Party has under international law ..."

[55] Article 4 establishes requirements for consultations "on exploration and exploitation activities" carried out within certain areas surrounding the Delimitation Line.

[56] Article 5 outlines a multi-step process for reaching a determination on the existence of a Transboundary Reservoir. This determination entails deadlines for consultations and submissions to the "Joint Commission" as defined elsewhere in the Agreement.

[57] Article 6 details the components of a Unitization Agreement, including requirements to measure production; procedures for ensuring accurate payments of royalties and other proceeds; and safety and environmental measures to be taken under the national laws of each party.

[58] Article 7 addresses management guidelines prior to the formation of a transboundary unit.

[59] Articles 8 and 9 provide for determining and redetermining allocation of production.

[60] Article 10 reads as follows: "The Executive Agencies shall ensure that a unit operator for a Transboundary Unit is designated by agreement between the Licensees. The designation or change of the unit operator shall be subject to the approval of the Executive Agencies. The unit operator will act on behalf of the Licensees."

[61] Articles 11 and 12 provide general guidelines addressing operational aspects of a project to facilitate cooperation between relevant parties.

[62] Article 13 provides the following: "Income arising from the Exploitation of Transboundary Reservoirs shall be taxed (continued...)

**Chapter 4** (Article 14) creates an institutional body for resolving disputes. This body is referred to as a Joint Commission.[63]

**Chapter 5** (Articles 15-17) details the process for dispute settlement by providing options for parties to resolve disagreements arising from implementation of the Agreement.[64]

**Chapter 6** (Articles 18-19) outlines principles for joint inspections relating to safety and environmental protection.[65]

**Chapter 7** (Articles 20-27) concludes the Agreement with a variety of provisions to guide the process for amending, terminating and bringing the Agreement into force,[66] terminating the moratorium[67] and determining how the Agreement might relate to other agreements.[68]

Consistent with both countries' stated intentions in 2010,[69] officials on both sides of the border have asserted that the Agreement achieves stated goals for "jointly managing, administering and governing" the transboundary area in a "considered, sustainable and structured manner" in order to "optimize energy resource development and to protect the surrounding marine environment."[70]

---

(...continued)

in accordance with the legislation of the United Mexican States and the United States of America respectively, as well as the Convention between the Government of the United States of America and the Government of the United Mexican States for the Avoidance of Double Taxation and the Prevention of Fiscal Evasion with respect to Taxes on Income and Capital, signed on September 18th, 1992, as amended (and as may be amended in the future), or any Convention superseding that Convention as the Parties may enter into in the future."

[63] Article 14 is more detailed than most other provisions in the Agreement. It refers to powers vested in the Joint Commission for resolving differences concerning the allocation of production pursuant to Articles 8 and 9. It sets deadlines for the Joint Commission to act and provides alternatives for resolving disputes.

[64] Articles 15, 16 and 17 provide broad guidelines for consultations, mediation, expert determination and arbitration. These guidelines include multiple references to deadlines and to terms defined elsewhere in the Agreement.

[65] Articles 18 and 19 generally reference "applicable national law" as a basis of joint inspections in the area.

[66] Articles 20, 21, 22, and 23 provide details about amending, terminating and bringing this Agreement into force.

[67] Article 24 reads as follows: "Upon entry into force of this Agreement, the period of any moratorium on the authorization or permitting of petroleum or natural gas drilling or exploration of the continental shelf within the boundary "Area" as established by Article 4, paragraph 1, of the 2000 Treaty on the Continental Shelf and extended by any subsequent exchanges of notes shall be terminated."

[68] Article 25 asserts that "nothing in this Agreement shall affect the rights and obligations of the Parties with respect to other international agreements to which they are both party."

[69] On June 23, 2010, a Joint Statement was adopted by President Obama and then-President Calderon at the conclusion of then-President Calderon's State Visit to Washington on May 19, 2010. For the full set of remarks, see http://www.whitehouse.gov/the-press-office/joint-statement-president-barack-obama-and-president-felipe-calder-n. See also *Joint Statement by President Barack Obama, President Felipe Calderon of Mexico, and Prime Minister Stephen Harper of Canada on Climate Change and Clean Energy* (August 10, 2009).

[70] For the full set of remarks at the signing of the U.S.-Mexico Transboundary Agreement, Los Cabos, Mexico, February 20, 2012, see http://www.state.gov/secretary/rm/2012/02/184236 htm.

---

# Possible Implications of Implementing Legislation[71]

Diplomats from the United States and Mexico have described possible implications of the Agreement entering into force as follows:

- The current moratorium on oil exploration and production would end.

- A cooperative process for managing the maritime boundary region would begin.

- It would be possible for commercial activities to unfold involving options for companies to voluntarily enter into unitization arrangements. In the event such an arrangement is not achieved, the Agreement also establishes options by which companies might develop potential resources on each side of the border.

- Joint inspection teams addressing compliance with applicable laws and regulations would be activated by both governments to review operational plans relevant to transboundary reservoirs.[72]

Parties on both sides of the border have observed that the Agreement does not provide specific details about a possible development scenario. Instead it offers a framework for both countries to work further to commence joint operations.

Other possible impacts on activities in the Gulf of Mexico or, from a broader perspective, on the national ocean energy portfolio remain a matter of conjecture.[73] For example, as part of estimating fiscal impacts, many in Congress turn to the Congressional Budget Office (CBO) score for H.R. 1613.[74] On May 17, 2013, CBO estimated that "enacting H.R. 1613 would increase offsetting receipts from offshore lease sales by $25 million from 2014 through 2023." As part of this analysis, CBO assumes, first, that approving the Agreement would allow DOI to offer leases for acreage which is currently under moratorium and, second, that approving the Agreement would increase values of other leased tracts in the nearby area.[75]

Other possible implications of the Agreement coming into force involve coping with challenges related to safety and monitoring marine borders; issues surrounding disbursement of potential revenue anticipated from U.S.-Mexico projects; and the concentration of undeveloped leases in the Gulf of Mexico. Each of these issues is discussed in the next section.

---

[71] Information used for this section was obtained from the U.S. Department of State Fact Sheet dated February 20, 2012, and found at http://www.state.gov/r/pa/prs/ps/2012/02/184235 htm.

[72] See joint statement adopted by Presidents Obama and Calderon, Washington, DC, May 19, 2010.

[73] Concurrent with regulating operations in the Gulf of Mexico, DOI is assessing energy resource potential off the coast of the Mid- and South Atlantic and off the coasts of California and Alaska, including in the Chukchi and Beaufort Seas. For a comprehensive statement of current federal policies toward offshore oil and gas development, see 77 *Federal Register* 40080 (July 6, 2012).

[74] For a full CBO report on H.R. 1613, see http://www.cbo.gov/sites/default/files/cbofiles/attachments/hr1613.pdf.

[75] For information about the lease sales referred to in the CBO score see Five-Year Outer Continental Shelf (OCS) Oil and Gas Leasing Program for 2012–2017, 77 *Federal Register* 40080 (July 6, 2012).

## What Is "Unitization?"

Unitization is a method to jointly develop a field or reservoir that might encompass a large area and even straddle a state or national boundary. This method for OCS development is common in U.S. waters. Described by some as the centerpiece of the Agreement, unitization facilitates companies licensed by the United States and by Mexico (through the state oil company Petróleos Mexicanos, PEMEX) to operate as one entity as part of joint operations involving distinct oil and gas reservoirs potentially discovered to extend across the maritime boundary.[76] Frameworks for unitization (including the framework adopted in the U.S.-Mexico Agreement) can be founded on a combination of the following:

- international law—formal agreements between countries (consistent with treaties, conventions and international customs);

- national laws of host governments, and contracts between host governments and licensees; and

- private contracts among licensees and interested third parties, such as operating agreements and production sales contracts.

An example of a project in U.S. waters made possible through unitization exists in the western Gulf of Mexico—the Perdido project. **Figure 7** illustrates this project by highlighting the three subsea units that tie back to a floating production facility referred to as a Regional Host. This facility is located in approximately 8,000 feet of water, approximately 250 miles south of Houston, TX, and less than 100 miles from the transboundary area cited in the Agreement. When first constructed, this project was the deepest "vertical access" facility in the world.[77]

## Figure 7. Perdido Host as Example of Unitization in the Western Gulf of Mexico

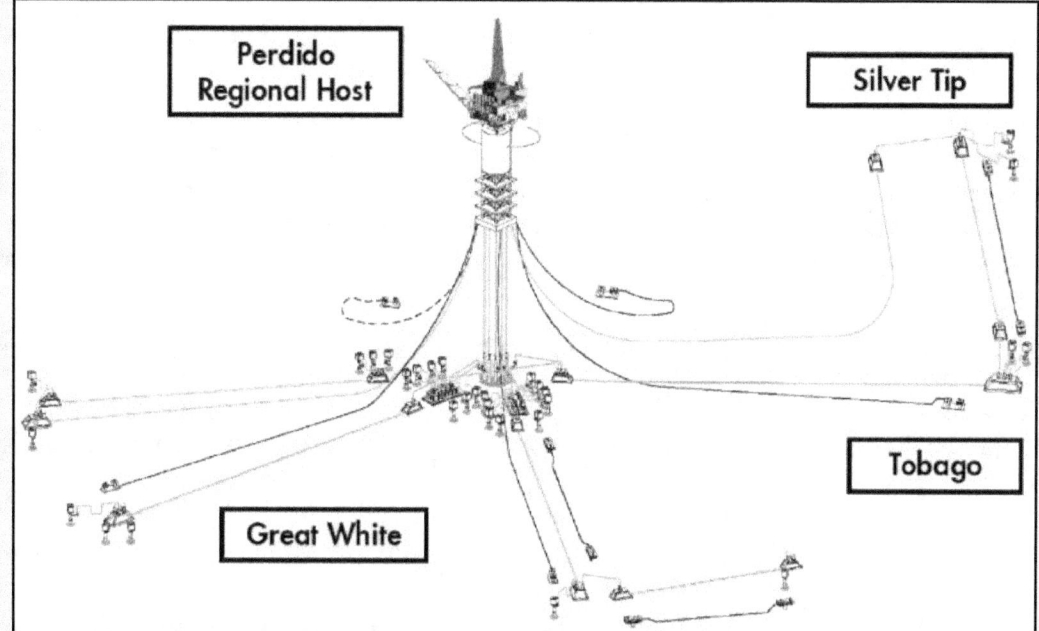

**Source:** Perdido Development System, modified by CRS.

---

[76] Transboundary Agreement, Articles 2, 6, 7, 8, 9, 10, 11, 12, 18, 22, 23. See also S.Rept. 112-43, *Oil Mexico, and the Transboundary Agreement*, Senate Committee on Foreign Relations (December 21, 2012). See also 30 CFR 250 Subpart M. See http://www.bsee.gov/Exploration-and-Production/Unitization/Unitization.aspx.

[77] A "vertical access" facility is a system comprising a floating host located over a drilling location with the floating host comprising drilling functions. More information on this facility can be found at http://www.shell.com.

---

# U.S. Perspectives and Issues for Congress

A number of developments have influenced review of the Agreement and subsequent legislative action by the 113th Congress. First, both governments have demonstrated an increased interest in developing ocean energy resources.[78] Second, the Mexican Senate moved swiftly to approve the Agreement on April 12, 2012, and the Mexican Presidency completed all other domestic requirements to implement the Agreement on May 22, 2012. Third, various U.S. stakeholders (some in the U.S. energy sector and some environmental organizations) have expressed interests related to the Agreement.[79] Further legislative action to implement the Agreement, if any, during the 113th Congress will likely also be influenced by the issues discussed below.

## Jointly Developing Ocean Energy Resources

Many Members of Congress and the Obama Administration have supported efforts to enhance U.S.-Mexico energy cooperation for several reasons, including enhancing energy supplies and energy security. Executive branch officials assert that U.S. interests benefit from jointly developing the transboundary area, particularly in light of Mexico's role as a key U.S. partner in other policy spheres (trade, border issues, international drug interdiction and law enforcement). They also assert that U.S.-Mexico cooperation will help manage ocean energy resources on both sides of the marine border by enhancing energy production while monitoring safety and environmental protection.

U.S. diplomatic officials have asserted that various commitments between the United States and Mexico protect U.S. interests in expanding options for developing hydrocarbons and that this Agreement merely updates and strengthens existing treaties between the two countries. At issue for some in Congress is whether implementing this U.S.-Mexico Agreement is an essential step in forming U.S.-Mexico partnerships relevant to generating energy supplies along marine borders.

## Disbursement of Revenue Anticipated from U.S.-Mexico Projects

U.S. officials usually seek to clarify the management of receipts and disbursements related to energy production as part of the earliest deliberations about options for developing ocean energy resources.[80]

---

[78] In the United States, the 110th Congress allowed the annual congressional moratoriums included in DOI appropriations acts to expire on September 30, 2008, and did not extend these congressional bans on oil and gas leasing activities (P.L. 110-329). Legislation related to domestic moratoriums has been driven by support for promoting domestic energy production to improve energy security, and increasing offshore receipts and disbursements.

[79] See statement of Nicolette Nye, spokeswoman for National Ocean Industries Association (NOIA) in "U.S.-Mexico transboundary Agreement mired in Congress," January 8, 2013, at http://www.eenews net/gw/sample/print/3. See statement of Greenpeace, "Transboundary Agreement Spells Disaster for the Gulf," February 22, 2012.

[80] In April 2009, the United States and Mexico touched on this and other themes as part of launching a comprehensive effort—the Bilateral Framework on Clean Energy and Climate Change—to explore ways to further develop the potential of an energy relationship. With its focus on renewable energy, energy efficiency, jobs and technology development, the Bilateral Framework has supported work on common standards, closer integration of electricity grids and other development goals in border regions.

Consistent with various revenue management mechanisms that have evolved over the years, an established percentage of federal revenues flows to federal and state projects in designated portions of the Gulf of Mexico.[81] In the past, determining an acceptable division of revenue from future offshore energy projects between coastal states and the federal government has proven to be a difficult problem. When leased tracts on federal territory are at issue, coastal states argue that they bear the brunt of remediating environmental impacts and infrastructure wear-and-tear accompanying offshore oil and gas activity. Some states also harbor concern about international development scenarios impacting shore-side communities and possibly increasing statewide costs related to water-dependent activities.

To date, OCS revenues have been a major source of funds for the Land and Water Conservation Fund (LWCF) and the National Historic Preservation Fund (NHPF).[82] State and federal entities use these funds to acquire park and recreational lands. Thus far, U.S. review of the Agreement has not examined values involved in an equitable distribution of public revenues, if any, related to offshore projects managed jointly by the United States and Mexico.

At issue for Congress is whether statutory mandates related to nation-to-nation or federal-state revenue-sharing programs might be considered as part of U.S. review of the Agreement.

## Worker Safety, Public Health, and Environmental Protection

Worker safety, public health, and environmental protection stemming from activities at marine border areas present special challenges, in part because international marine borders tend to be geographically remote, resulting in limited options for equipment inspections, audits of worker training, and law enforcement coverage.[83] These concerns about activities in offshore areas are relevant to safety, health, and environmental protection issues onshore because of the nature of air- and waterborne pollutants and debris. At marine border areas, oil and gas facilities are subject to regulation by the Bureau of Safety and Environmental Enforcement (BSEE), the DOI agency responsible for federal inspections and reviewing oil spill response plans; and testing oil spill containment equipment.[84]

While marine border activities may be governed by different federal missions (military, diplomatic, trade) and involve various federal or international jurisdictions, agencies have been required to integrate planning and regulatory compliance requirements to ensure that federal

---

[81] See Gulf of Mexico Energy Security Act of 2006 (GOMESA, P.L. 109-432).

[82] The LWCF is a trust fund that accumulates $900 million at the end of each fiscal year. While most of the $900 million is derived from offshore revenues, additional monies have been provided by surplus property sales, and DOI fees otherwise collected from public lands. The National Historic Preservation Act of 1966 establishes the Historic Preservation Fund, made up annually of monies intended for matching grants to the states and to the National Trust for Historic Preservation. These funds are not administered as typical "trust funds." Both consist of monies that cannot be spent unless appropriated by Congress. From FY1965 through FY2012, less than half the accumulated funds in the LWCF have been appropriated. For more information, see CRS Report RL33531, *Land and Water Conservation Fund: Overview, Funding History, and Issues*, by Carol Hardy Vincent.

[83] U.S. Government Accountability Office, *Border Security: Additional Actions Needed to Better Ensure a Coordinated Federal Response to Illegal Activity on Federal Lands*, GAO-11-177, November 2010, pp. 9-10.

[84] The Bureau of Safety and Environmental Enforcement (BSEE, pronounced "*Bessy*") is tasked with DOI oversight and enforcement for offshore field operations, inspections, workforce safety, and decommissioning. Other than BSEE authorities pursuant to OCSLA, BSEE responsibilities are governed by the National Environmental Policy Act of 1969 (NEPA P.L. 91-190; 42 U.S.C. §§ 4321-4347 and implementing regulations 40 C.F.R. Part 1500.

---

decisions reflect values Americans place on worker safety and environmental protection.[85] Sometimes departments—including DOI, for example—have signed memoranda of understanding (MOUs) on border issues that govern information sharing related to safety, budgeting, and access to federal lands, among other topics.[86]

Of particular interest to some in Congress might be how legislative initiatives discussed above might ensure safety at the marine border by detailing strategies to address worker safety and environmental protection.

## Concentration of Non-Producing Leases in the Gulf of Mexico

Continuous federal oil and gas leasing in the Gulf of Mexico from the 1950s to the present has contributed to a higher concentration of federal leases in the Gulf of Mexico region than in the other three regions (Atlantic, Pacific and Alaska) combined. DOI reports that most federally regulated leases in the Gulf of Mexico remain undeveloped (showing no physical signs of development). While the leases might generate rental receipts and values related to assignments and transfers, currently these leases generate neither energy supplies nor royalties.[87]

An issue attracting increased attention among some in Congress is how to cope with new leasing options when so many leased tracts already exist. Some concerned about the number of non-producing U.S. leases question the benefits of leasing more acreage without examining the significance, if any, of the backlog of undeveloped leased tracts. Others contend that with no statutory limit on the number of undeveloped leases a leaseholder may own, there should be no correlation between new leasing options and efforts to examine (or reduce) the number of non-producing leases.

Disagreements related to so-called "idle leases" can stem from differing perspectives on the values attached to the oil and gas leasing system in the U.S. Gulf of Mexico. Arguably, the value of each lease (producing and non-producing) is determined by the company owning the lease. In theory, all leases might play a role on an owner's balance sheet. Some leases might not be producing energy supplies or public revenue, but they provide operational and investment options for the leaseholder. These options that might include rights-of-way, access to credit through liens or mortgages, or other attributes derived from accounting rules or the tax code.[88]

Attention to this issue has a tendency to wax and wane, with lawmaker interest increasing in recent years.

---

[85] For more information on compliance with NEPA in relation to U.S. border programs, see CBP, "SBI Environmental Documents," http://www.cbp.gov/xp/cgov/border_security/otia/sbi_news/sbi_enviro_docs/. A related issue is the authority, and litigation challenging the authority, related to waivers from environmental protection statutes.

[86] For information on issues related to border barriers, see CRS Report R42138, *Border Security: Immigration Enforcement Between Ports of Entry*, by Marc R. Rosenblum.

[87] In the absence of physical development, other than company disclosures and agency lease tenure records, there is little to indicate the role these leases play in the offshore ocean energy program. GAO, *Oil and Gas Leasing: Interior Could Do More to Encourage Diligent Development*, GAO-09-74 (Washington, D.C.: Oct. 3, 2008). See also *Oil and Gas Lease Utilization, Onshore and Offshore*, Updated Report to the President DOI (May 2012).

[88] In theory, important tax implications can stem from how taxpayers with OCS leases determine their value. Specifically, the character of any losses or gains (e.g., capital asset or ordinary income, carried interest) associated with OCS leases could, in theory, be a factor for some firms maintaining an increasing number of undeveloped tracts.

# Conclusion

Controversy surrounds most U.S. legislative initiatives to grant (or defer) offshore oil and gas drilling rights. A persistent question among lawmakers is how to cope with myriad issues and competing interests at stake when it comes to managing ocean resources.[89] Of the breadth of issues and interests that might be related to proposed legislation to implement the U.S.-Mexico Transboundary Hydrocarbons Agreement, this report focuses on resource management issues, only addressing the competing national interests that mainly involve balancing the demands of producing ocean energy supplies while protecting marine and coastal resources and resources found beyond the U.S. EEZ.

While the Obama Administration has stated that the Agreement is part of engaging Mexico in a host of related energy and environmental partnerships, asserting that the benefits of this Agreement outweigh potential risks, skeptics have voiced doubt that the Agreement ensures an emphasis on rigorous safety measures on both sides of the border.[90] Related issues include how to handle public receipts (royalties and other gains), if any, anticipated from jointly managed ocean energy projects and how to cope with oil spill risks and other risks associated with a joint development scenario.

Recent activities in the House and Senate highlight increased interest in implementing the Agreement. In the House, debate underscored a policy divide that accompanies legislative review of this Agreement.[91] Arguably, positions expressed about legislation to accept and implement the Agreement reflect two camps: one focusing on the benefits of maintaining the moratorium on ocean drilling and the other focusing on gains anticipated from options to generate new energy supplies and public revenues.

Some of these arguments highlight external factors associated with U.S.-Mexico relations.[92] However, most arguments are reminiscent of the historic choices faced by U.S. lawmakers in the past about whether and where to allow ocean drilling and how to monitor development scenarios where permissible.

As the expiration of the moratorium draws closer, pressure may increase for lawmakers and diplomatic officials on both sides of the border to find an acceptable policy alternative for achieving a safe, responsible, and sustainable future for U.S. and Mexican ocean energy portfolios in the Gulf of Mexico. With no schedule in place for further U.S. review of the Agreement, it is difficult to predict whether Congress might defer attention to the Agreement or undertake further U.S. review.

---

[89] The offshore drilling debate is a combination of several discrete debates about oil and gas leasing activity in federal and international waters. Congress addresses multiple issues related to access (state-federal consultations about state revenue sharing, adequacy of environmental reviews, timetables for drilling permitting, operational safety, federal receipts and disbursements to federal programs, research).

[90] See, for example, Greenpeace, *Transboundary Agreement Spells Disaster for the Gulf,* February 22, 2012.

[91] H.Rept. 113-101, including Dissenting Views.

[92] For a comprehensive discussion of U.S.-Mexican relations see CRS Report R42917, *Mexico's Peña Nieto Administration: Priorities and Key Issues in U.S.-Mexican Relations,* by Clare Ribando Seelke.

# Appendix. Summary of Congressional Hearings

Both House hearings discussed below were conducted prior to lawmakers introducing the bills discussed elsewhere in this report. Absent the opportunity to parse introduced legislation, witnesses mainly offered general statements relevant to the Agreement. As a result these hearings were free of the more precise legislative analysis and stakeholder discussion that can come from review directly related to pending legislation.[93]

## House Committee on Foreign Affairs

On March 14, 2013, the House Committee on Foreign Affairs, Subcommittee on the Western Hemisphere held a hearing entitled *U.S. Energy Security: Enhancing Partnerships with Mexico and Canada*.[94] At the hearing the four witnesses representing academia and private sector firms[95] claimed U.S. approval of the Agreement would impact U.S. and Mexican interests through one or more of the following considerations:

- "Approving the treaty will create new levels of legal certainty for U.S. and Mexican firms operating in the Gulf border regions, encouraging them to engage in the risk-taking required to produce oil from deep waters ... "[96]

- "Swift ratification of the Transboundary Hydrocarbon Agreement is important to our nation's energy security and long-term economic growth."[97]

- "The current focus on hydrocarbon reform in Mexico also means that extended U.S. inaction on the Transboundary Hydrocarbons Agreement will be noticed, with potentially negative consequences for the broader bilateral relationship."[98]

## House Committee on Natural Resources

On April 25, 2013, the House Committee on Natural Resources, Subcommittee on Energy and Mineral Resources held a legislative and oversight hearing entitled "*U.S.-Mexico Transboundary Hydrocarbon Agreement and Steps Needed for Implementation*."[99] At this hearing six witnesses representing federal agencies, private firms, academia, and an internationally recognized

---

[93] This Agreement has been characterized as very technical in nature, as compared to earlier U.S.-Mexico compacts related to governance of acreage in western Gulf of Mexico. For a discussion detailing the technical aspects of the Agreement see *U.S.-Mexico Agreement on Transboundary Hydrocarbon Reservoirs in the Gulf of Mexico: A Blueprint for Progress or a Recipe for Conflict?* by Jorge A Vargas, (San Diego International Law Journal Fall, 2012).

[94] See http://foreignaffairs.house.gov/hearing/subcommittee-hearing-us-energy-security-enhancing-partnerships-mexico-and-canada.

[95] Witnesses included Duncan Wood, Ph.D., Director, Mexico Institute, The Wilson Center; Daniel R. Simmons, Director of Regulatory and State Affairs, Institute for Energy Research; Kyle Isakower, Vice President, Regulatory and Economic Policy, American Petroleum Institute; Michael A. Levi, Ph.D., Senior Fellow for Energy and the Environment, and Director of the Program on Energy Security and Climate Change, Council on Foreign Relations. No Administration witness was on the panel.

[96] Testimony of Duncan Wood.

[97] Testimony of Kyle Isakower.

[98] Testimony of Michael Levi.

[99] See http://foreignaffairs.house.gov/hearing/subcommittee-hearing-us-energy-security-enhancing-partnerships-mexico-and-canada.

---

environmental organization offered perspectives on U.S. involvement in the Agreement.[100] With one exception, witnesses voiced support for the Agreement and draft legislation, by claiming that U.S. acceptance of the Agreement offered greater legal certainty for U.S. energy interests in the Gulf of Mexico. The one exception was Mr. Manuel, Sierra Club, arguing that the Agreement was not needed due to the backlog of U.S. leases already in effect in the Gulf of Mexico.[101] Witnesses asserted varying perspectives on the Agreement, based on one or more of the following considerations:

- The Agreement permits, for the first time, firms on the U.S. side of the border to cooperate with Mexico's national oil company, Petróleos Mexicanos (PEMEX) on joint exploration and development projects.[102]

- The Agreement allows more numerous options for U.S. oil and natural gas companies to invest in and to operate in the Gulf of Mexico, creating jobs and enhancing U.S. energy security.[103]

- Lacking specifics about safety and environmental protection, it remains unclear whether the Agreement is compatible with U.S. interests in fishing and tourism in the Gulf of Mexico.[104]

Of the witnesses testifying in favor of legislative review and acceptance of the Agreement, each cited clarifying U.S.-Mexico relations with respect to governing the transboundary area was needed for safe and responsible energy development to commence. In contrast to the testimony of these witnesses, the Sierra Club witness expressed skepticism that swift U.S. acceptance was needed "given that the oil and gas industry is sitting on a large number of inactive leases in federal waters, proving accelerated leasing in the Gulf of Mexico to be unnecessary."[105]

Following these hearings, legislation (S. 812, H.R. 1613) was introduced in both chambers on April 25, 2013. This legislation would approve and implement the Agreement taking slightly differing approaches.[106]

---

[100] Witnesses included Tommy Beaudreau, Acting Assistant Secretary for Land and Minerals Management U.S. Department of the Interior (DOI); Ambassador Carlos Pascual, Special Envoy and Coordinator for International Energy Affairs U.S. Department of State (DOS); Erik Milito, American Petroleum Institute; Daniel R. Simmons, Institute for Energy Research; Steven Groves, Heritage Foundation; and, Athan Manuel, Sierra Club.

[101] Sierra Club statement is found at http://naturalresources.house.gov/uploadedfiles/manueltestimony04-25-13.pdf.

[102] This point was made by both Mr. Beaudreau (DOI) and Ambassador Pascual (DOS). For the complete written testimony of both witnesses see http://naturalresources.house.gov/uploadedfiles/beaudreautestimony04-25-13.pdf and http://naturalresources.house.gov/uploadedfiles/pascualtestimony04-25-13.pdf.

[103] This point was made by both Mr. Milito and Mr. Groves. For the complete written testimony of both witnesses see http://naturalresources.house.gov/uploadedfiles/militotestimony04-25-13.pdf and http://naturalresources.house.gov/uploadedfiles/grovestestimony04-25-13.pdf.

[104] This point was made by Mr. Manuel. For the complete Sierra Club statement see http://naturalresources.house.gov/uploadedfiles/manueltestimony04-25-13.pdf.

[105] See Sierra Club written testimony, p. 3. For further information on offshore acreage leased but not producing see *Oil and Gas Lease Utilization – Onshore and Offshore*, Report to the President, U.S. Department of the Interior (March, 2011) found at http://www.doi.gov/news/pressreleases/loader.cfm?csModule=security/getfile&pageid=239255.

[106] These bills are summarized in the section of this report entitled "Pending Legislation."

---

### *Senate Committee on Energy and Natural Resources*

On October 1, 2013, the Senate Committee on Energy and Natural Resources held a legislative hearing on S. 812 and H.R. 1613, as part of examining the proper federal management role relevant to transboundary hydrocarbon reservoirs, and for other purposes. Government witnesses[107] offered testimony consistent with support for implementing the Agreement. Private sector witnesses offered testimony expressing opposing views: industry supporting the implementing legislation and environmental groups expressing objections.[108] The following highlights describe hearing testimony:

- Without the Agreement, firms on both sides of the border will likely not explore and develop deepwater projects of interest to both countries.[109]

- The Agreement allows for more legal certainty for all parties with a stake in planning offshore development scenarios. Many perceive this added certainty as creating a more favorable business atmosphere for U.S. oil and natural gas companies seeking to finance operations in the Gulf of Mexico.[110]

- Lacking detailed provisions related to safety and environmental protection in the Agreement, lifting the current moratorium is premature and raises concerns about pollution events including increased Green House Gas (GHG) emissions and oil spills that could jeopardize U.S. fishing, tourism and other interests in the Gulf of Mexico and elsewhere.[111]

The timing of this hearing and public admission to the hearing were affected by the Senate experiencing the first day of the federal government shutdown.[112] After this hearing the Senate Committee on Energy and Natural Resources discharged S. 812 by unanimous consent. On October 12, 2013, the Senate passed S. 812, without amendment, by unanimous consent.

---

[107] Ambassador Carlos Pascual, Special Envoy and Coordinator, International Energy Affairs, U.S. Department of State and Tommy P. Beaudreau, Acting Assistant Secretary, Land and Minerals Management, DOI.

[108] Ms. Jacqueline Savitz, Vice President, U.S. Oceans, Oceana expressed opposition to both bills; Mr. Erik Milito, Director, Upstream and Industry Operations, expressed American Petroleum Institute support for the legislation.

[109] This point was made by Mr. Beaudreau (DOI) and Ambassador Pascual (DOS) and Mr. Milito. For the complete written testimony of these witnesses see http://www.energy.senate.gov/public/index.cfm/2013/10/full-committee-hearing-to-consider-s-812-and-h-r-1613.

[110] This point was made by both government and industry witnesses.

[111] This point was made by Ms. Savitz. For the complete Oceana statement see http://www.energy.senate.gov/public/index.cfm/files/serve?File_id=4acfb140-c30a-4baf-9513-710733d3c945.

[112] CRS Report RL34680, *Shutdown of the Federal Government: Causes, Processes, and Effects*, coordinated by Clinton T. Brass.

---

# Author Contact Information

Curry L. Hagerty
Specialist in Energy and Natural Resources Policy
chagerty@crs.loc.gov, 7-7738

James C. Uzel
Geospatial Information Systems Analyst
juzel@crs.loc.gov, 7-6830